NATIONAL GEOGRAPHIC

The Pueblos

People of the Southwest

A HISTORICAL LOOK AT NATIVE AMERICANS

Ruby Maile

PICTURE CREDITS
Cover: © Horace Bristol/Corbis/Tranz

page 1 © Corbis/Tranz; page 5 (top) © Getty Images; page 7
© Adam Woolfitt/Corbis/Tranz; page 8 (top) © Corbis/Tranz; page 8
(bottom) © Getty Images; page 10 © Corbis/Tranz; page 11
© Corbis/Tranz; page 12 © Wolfgang Kaehler/Corbis/Tranz; page
13 © Dave G. Houser/Corbis/Tranz; page 14 © Corbis/Tranz; page
15 © Adam Woolfitt/Corbis/Tranz; page 16 © Pete
Saloutos/Corbis/Tranz; page 18 © Buddy Mays/Corbis/Tranz;
page 21, 23 © Mark Sublette, Medicine Man Gallery; page 24
© Velino Shije Herrera. National Cowboy & Western Heritage
Museum, Oklahoma City, OK; page 26 © Velino Shije Herrera.
Pueblo Buffalo Dancers. Ink on paper, 1996.27.0442. National
Cowboy & Western Heritate Museum, Oklahoma City, OK; Outside
back cover: (top left) © Christie's Images/Corbis/Tranz; (top right)
© Horace Bristol/Corbis/Tranz; (bottom left)
© Bettman/Corbis/Tranz; (bottom right) © National Anthropological
Archives, Smithsonian Institute, T.W. Smillie, Neg 73-9466.

Produced through the worldwide resources of the National
Geographic Society, John M. Fahey, Jr., President and Chief
Executive Officer; Gilbert M. Grosvenor, Chairman of the Board;
Nina D. Hoffman, Executive Vice President and President, Books
and Education Publishing Group.

PREPARED BY NATIONAL GEOGRAPHIC SCHOOL PUBLISHING
Ericka Markman, Senior Vice President and President, Children's
Books and Education Publishing Group; Steve Mico, Vice President
and Editorial Director; Marianne Hiland, Executive Editor; Richard
Easby, Editorial Manager; Jim Hiscott, Design Manager; Kristin
Hanneman, Illustrations Manager; Matt Wascavage, Manager of
Publishing Services; Sean Philpotts, Production Manager.

EDITORIAL MANAGEMENT
Morrison BookWorks, LLC

PROGRAM CONSULTANTS
Dr. Shirley V. Dickson, Program Director, Literacy, Education
Commission of the States; Margit E. McGuire, Ph.D., Professor of
Teacher Education and Social Studies, Seattle University.

CONTENT REVIEWER
Glenabah Martinez, Ph.D., Taos Pueblo, University of New Mexico.

National Geographic Theme Sets program developed by Macmillan
Education Australia, Pty Limited.

Published by the National Geographic Society
1145 17th Street, N.W.
Washington, D.C. 20036-4688

ISBN: 0-7922-4727-2

Product 41967

Printed in Hong Kong.

Contents

A Historical Look at Native Americans

Native Americans have lived in the United States for thousands of years, long before other peoples made their homes here. There are many different Native American nations or peoples, each with their own language, traditions, and way of life. These peoples include the Nez Perce, the Pueblos, the Iroquois, and the Cheyenne.

 ## Key Concepts ....

1. **The homelands of native people have influenced their food, clothing, and shelter.**

2. **The stories and arts of native people were an expression of culture and a way of passing on values.**

3. **Early trade was a way of exchanging both goods and ideas.**

Native American Homelands of Long Ago

The Nez Perce

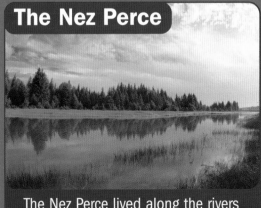

The Nez Perce lived along the rivers of the Northwest.

The Pueblos

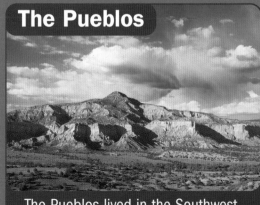

The Pueblos lived in the Southwest.

This Pueblo man, Ray Mirabal, once lived in Taos Pueblo. In this book you will read about the history of the Pueblo people.

The Iroquois

The Iroquois lived surrounded by the woods of the Northeast.

The Cheyenne

The Cheyenne lived on the flat grasslands of the central Plains.

The PUEBLOS:
People of the Southwest

The Pueblos are a Native American people. Many groups belong to the Pueblos, including the Hopi and the Zunis. When the Spanish came to the Southwest 400 years ago, they named the Native American villages "**pueblos**."

The word pueblo is the Spanish word for "village." This is how the Native Americans of this region became known as Pueblos.

Key Concept 1 The homelands of native people have influenced their food, clothing, and shelter.

The Homeland of the Pueblos

The **homeland** of the Pueblo people is the southwestern area of the United States. It is the area where the Pueblo people first lived. Many Pueblo groups still live there today. This area covers parts of Arizona and New Mexico.

homeland
the place a people or nation chooses to make its home

The Southwest is a beautiful place to live. The land and climate are varied. There are steep-walled canyons, flat **plateaus**, and sandy deserts. Some parts of the Southwest are hot and dry. In other parts there is a large amount of rain and even snow in the winter.

Most of the Pueblo people live near the Colorado River or the Rio Grande. *Rio grande* is Spanish for "big river."

The Rio Grande in New Mexico

Location of Pueblo Homeland

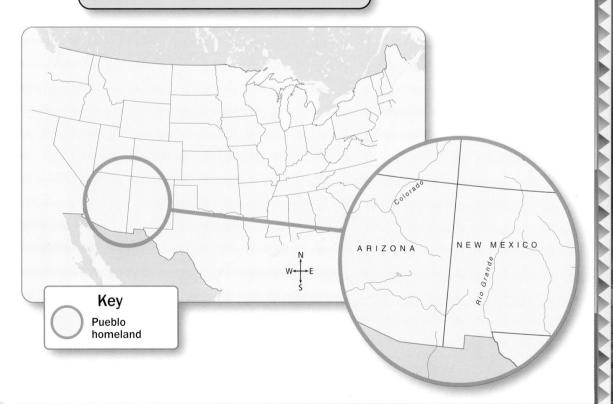

Key

Pueblo homeland

Colorado

ARIZONA   NEW MEXICO

Rio Grande

N
W   E
S

Food

The Pueblo people grew most of their food. They ate foods that grew well in the Southwest climate. Their main foods were corn, squash, beans, and peppers. Pueblo people still eat and prepare foods as they did long ago.

Pueblo people grew more than 20 different types of corn. The corn was dried in the open air. Then it was ground into cornmeal. Two heavy stones were used to grind the corn.

This Hopi girl has ground corn to make cornmeal.

The Pueblos also gathered some of their food. They gathered nuts and other wild plants. The fruit of most cactus plants could be eaten. This included the prickly pear. Gathering was difficult because food was not always available.

The Spanish taught the Pueblo people how to make ovens. The Pueblos still use these ovens to bake bread.

Farming

The Pueblo people were great farmers. They developed special methods to farm their lands. They planted corn deep into the ground so that it could use underground water to grow. They only **tilled** the top layer of soil. This helped the soil below remain wet.

Hunting

Hunting was the men's job. Pueblo hunters used bows and arrows, spears, and throwing sticks. They hunted deer, antelope, and rabbits. Sometimes they traveled into the Plains to hunt bison. They also hunted birds for their feathers. They used the feathers in ceremonies and to decorate their clothes.

The Pueblos hunted antelope for their meat and hides.

Pueblo Food Sources

Food Source	Spring	Summer	Fall	Winter
Fishing			✔	✔
Hunting	✔	✔		
Gathering	✔	✔		
Eating stored food			✔	✔

Clothing

The Pueblo people wore clothes made from what they found and hunted in their homeland. They used rabbit fur, deerskin, feathers, and cotton. Later, Spanish settlers brought sheep to the Southwest. Then, the Pueblo people began to use wool to make clothes.

The weather influenced what Pueblo people wore. When it was hot, Pueblo people wore light-weight clothes. When it was cold, they wore warmer clothes. They sewed animal skins together to make warm robes. The feathers from turkeys were used for decoration.

The Pueblo people also wove blankets, which they used as coverings when the weather was cold.

This Pueblo man is wearing a traditional woven blanket.

Men's Clothing

Pueblo men often wore a type of skirt or kilt, or else full-length cotton pants. A loose cotton shirt and deerskin **moccasins** were part of everyday wear.

Women's Clothing

Pueblo women often wore belted, knee-length, cotton dresses tied at the shoulder. They wore leggings and ankle-high moccasins made from animal skins. Women also wore ornaments made from wood, bone, and shell. Sometimes they made ornaments from a blue-green stone called **turquoise**.

These Pueblo women are wearing plain cotton dresses tied at the shoulder.

Shelter

The Pueblo people used the materials around them to build houses. They built houses that would keep them cool in summer and warm in winter.

Most houses were made of **adobe** bricks. Adobe is a mix of mud and straw. Most houses had a door in the roof. The people used a ladder to get down into the house. Then they pulled the ladder in behind them to stop enemies from coming in.

The Pueblos also had separate underground rooms called **kivas**. Kivas were used as a meeting place. Important information was passed on to the young people in the kivas. Many religious ceremonies took place there. Kivas are still used this way today.

Adobe buildings in Taos Pueblo, New Mexico

Language and Storytelling

Because the Pueblos are a group of many different peoples, they speak many different languages. The languages are **dialects**. This means they are similar but not exactly the same.

Telling stories and legends of the past is an important part of Pueblo life. Legends are traditional stories. These stories are meant to teach and to entertain. Elders pass on these stories to each new **generation**. Often, children sit in a circle around a storyteller who tells them stories. Telling stories helps to preserve **culture** and history.

culture
the traditions, language, dress, ceremonies, and other ways of life that a group of people share

In the past, the Pueblo people carved or painted their stories onto rocks and kiva walls.

Ancient Pueblo rock drawings, Albuquerque, New Mexico

Arts and Crafts

Arts and crafts have always been an important part of Pueblo life. In early times, the Pueblo people used cottonwood to weave baskets. The baskets were so tightly woven that they could even hold water.

Later, the people began using coils of wet clay to make clay pots. This way of making pots is still used by the Pueblos today. Pueblo potters roll the clay into snake shapes. Then they coil the snake shapes on top of each other to make a pot shape. Next, they use a smoothing stone to smooth the edges.

To make the clay hard, the potters first put the pots on stones. Then they pile wood around the pots. They burn the wood. The heat from the fire sets the clay and makes it hard. Once the pots are ready, the Pueblos paint traditional designs on them.

These Pueblo women are decorating traditional Pueblo pottery.

Key Concept 3 Early trade was a way of exchanging both goods and ideas.

Trade

Trade among the Native American people was common. Many Pueblo people in the Southwest traded with each other. They also traded with other Native American people from the Great Plains region in the North and from Mexico in the South. When the Spanish arrived, the Pueblos began trading with them as well.

Trade between Native Americans

Trade gatherings were held at least once a year. Many Native Americans met at these gatherings to trade their **goods**. The Pueblos traded baskets, pottery, and rabbit-fur blankets. They also traded salt, corn, beans, squash, and turquoise. In exchange for these goods, the Pueblos got meat, animal hides, shells, and parrots.

Today, the Pueblo people still make and sell turquoise jewelry.

The Pueblos and the Navajo

Around the fifteenth century, another group, the Navajo people, began settling in the Southwest region. The Navajo came from the Northwest. At first the Navajo were hunters. The Pueblo people began to influence the Navajo in many ways. The Pueblos taught the Navajo farming and weaving.

This Navajo woman is weaving. The Navajo people of today use weaving skills they learned from the Pueblos.

Trade with Europeans

When the Spanish people arrived from Europe, they brought horses with them. The horses changed the way that the Pueblos lived. The Pueblos used horses to carry heavy loads. Before they had horses, they had to carry things on their backs or use dogs to pull small loads.

Think About the **Key Concepts**

Think about what you read. Think about the pictures and charts. Use these to answer the questions. Share what you think with others.

1. How did the homeland of the Native Americans affect their life there?

2. Why was storytelling important?

3. What was special about the culture, or way of life, of this Native American group?

4. How did trade affect the Native American group discussed in this book?

Comparison Chart

A chart allows you to find specific facts quickly and easily.
You can learn new ideas without having to read many words.
Charts use words and a box-like layout to present ideas.

There are different kinds of charts.
This chart of Pueblo clothing is a comparison chart. It compares
different types of clothing and what they were made of.

How to Read a Comparison Chart

1. Read the title.

The title tells you the subject, or what the chart is about.

2. Read the column headings.

Columns go from top to bottom. The heading at the top of each
column tells you what kind of information is in the column.

3. Read the row headings.

Rows go from side to side. The headings in the left column name
items you will get information about as you read across each row.

4. Connect the information as you read.

Read across each row to find information about a subject. Read
down each column to compare information.

Pueblo Clothing

Type of Clothing	Deerskin	Fur	Cotton	Wool	Feathers
Shirts			✔		
Dresses			✔	✔	
Breechcloths	✔				
Pants			✔		
Robes	✔	✔			✔
Moccasins	✔				

What's in the Chart?

Read the chart by following the steps on page 18. Write a few sentences about Pueblo clothing. Compare your sentences with what another student wrote.

Biographical Sources

The purpose of **biographical sources** is to give information about people's lives.

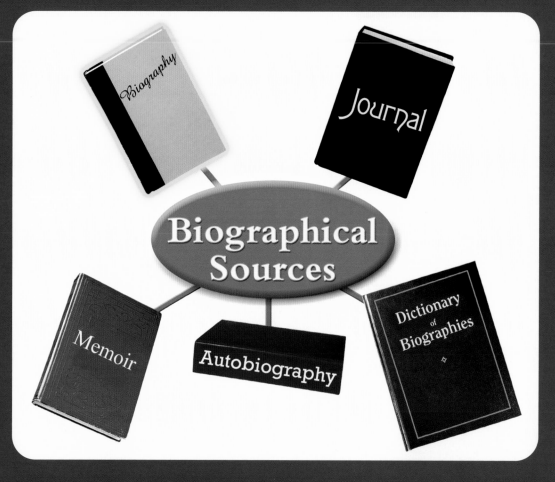

We read different biographical sources for different reasons. For example, if you want to read the story of someone's life, read a **biography**. But if you want to read one person's account of his or her own life, read that person's **autobiography**. Journals and memoirs are forms of autobiographies.

Pueblo Biographies

A biography tells the story of a person's life. The story is often told in the order in which things happened. This order is called chronological order. The following biographies are of Pueblo people.

Maria Martinez (1887–1980)

Name of the person

Dates tell of birth and death.

Maria Martinez

Maria Martinez lived her life by a few simple words. These words were, "Keep on the Indian Way." Eleanor Roosevelt, the wife of American President Franklin Roosevelt, said those words to Maria.

Just as many Pueblo people before her had done, Maria Martinez used clay to make pots. By doing this, she became famous.

Maria Martinez was born in 1887 in San Ildefonso (pronounced *ill-dee-fon-so*) Pueblo in New Mexico. The people of San Ildefonso Pueblo speak Tewa.

Photographs and illustrations show the person at various times in his or her life.

Text has details about the person's life.

Maria's father was a farmer and, as a child, she helped him around the farm. Maria went to school in the city of Santa Fe. She could speak English, Spanish, and Tewa.

When Maria was small, making clay pots was no longer a part of daily life. People were starting to forget the art of pottery making. This is because inexpensive Spanish metalware was easily available at the market. But Maria was interested in learning how pots were made.

Maria's aunt, Nicolasa, was a potter. As a child, Maria watched her aunt making pots. By watching, Maria learned to make pots. Nicolasa did not use a potter's wheel. Instead, she built pot shapes out of hand-coiled ribbons of clay. This was an ancient Pueblo way of making pots. Maria, too, made pots this way. She became an expert potter.

In 1904, Maria married Julian Martinez. Julian was a painter. Maria made the pots and Julian painted them. Soon after her marriage, Maria was contacted by the director of the Museum of New Mexico. He asked her to make old Pueblo-style pottery for the museum. Maria and Julian worked together on this project.

> As a child, Maria watched her aunt making pots. By watching, Maria learned to make pots.

A **Timeline** shows key events in the person's life.

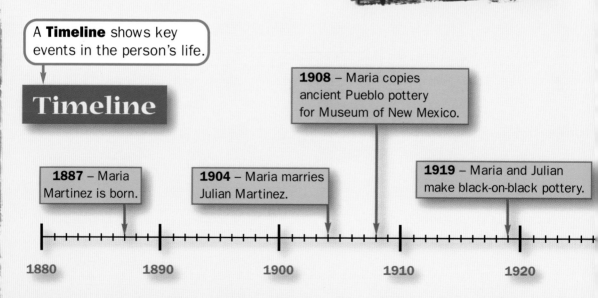

Timeline

1908 – Maria copies ancient Pueblo pottery for Museum of New Mexico.

1887 – Maria Martinez is born.

1904 – Maria marries Julian Martinez.

1919 – Maria and Julian make black-on-black pottery.

| 1880 | 1890 | 1900 | 1910 | 1920 |

Maria and Julian invented a new type of black-on-black pottery. One area of the pottery could have a dull finish and another area could be glossy black. The pottery also had designs painted in black. This style soon became very famous. People from all over America came to buy these pots.

Maria and Julian taught others in the village how to make their new style of pottery. Many people earned a living from making these pots. The pots are very valuable today and many people collect them.

This plate is an example of Maria's black-on-black pottery.

Maria Martinez teaching a pottery class

1943 – Julian Martinez dies. Maria and daughter-in-law Santana make pottery. Santana puts designs on Maria's pots.

1980 – Maria Martinez dies.

| 1940 | 1950 | 1960 | 1970 | 1980 |

Velino Shije Herrera (1902-1973)

Velino Shije Herrera

Velino Shije Herrera was born in 1902. His native name was Ma Pe Wi, which means "Oriole," or "Red Bird." He belonged to the Zia Pueblo of New Mexico. When Herrera was young, he went to Santa Fe Indian Boarding School. There he met a woman named Elizabeth De Huff. Elizabeth De Huff gave some students, including Herrera, art lessons after school. She encouraged them to draw and paint. Herrera decided to become a painter.

Herrera painted many pictures showing Pueblo life and customs. Some people of the Zia Pueblo did not like Herrera's paintings. They did not want him to paint pictures of their dances. But Herrera wanted to record the dresses and symbols of his culture. So, he continued to paint.

In one of his paintings, Herrera painted the Zia sun symbol. The state of New Mexico wanted to use this design as the state symbol. State officials asked Herrera for permission and Herrera agreed.

New Mexico's state flag features Herrera's drawing of the Zia sun symbol.

Herrera's design can be seen on the state flag, seal, and license plates of New Mexico. Some people of the Zia Pueblo were angry with Herrera. They did not want other people to use their traditional symbols.

Herrera's paintings were exhibited in North America and Europe. He is best known for his paintings of landscapes and hunting scenes. Herrerra also did many illustrations for books and taught art at the Albuquerque Indian School.

From 1931 to 1933, a large exhibition of Native American art toured the United States. The purpose of the exhibition was to show people many different forms of Native American art. Herrera's paintings were included in this exhibition.

In 1936, Herrera set up a studio in Santa Fe. This was a place where he painted and where people could come to see his paintings.

Most of Herrera's paintings use a lot of detail to show people and their clothing. Herrera used black outlines and then filled them in with strong blocks of color. He also did black and white drawings of Pueblo life, such as the picture below.

In 1956, Herrera's wife died in a car accident, and Herrera was injured. He did not paint much after that. Herrera's paintings continue to be displayed in museums across North America.

Herrera painted many pictures showing Pueblo life and customs.

Herrera drew pictures of traditional dancers like these Pueblo Buffalo Dancers.

Apply the **Key Concepts**

Key Concept 1 The homelands of native people have influenced their food, clothing, and shelter.

Activity

Choose three items the Pueblos found or hunted in their homeland. Make a sketch of each of these items using this book and other sources as references. Then use arrows and labels to tell how the Pueblos used these items in their daily lives.

antelope

meat for food

Key Concept 2 The stories and arts of native people were an expression of culture and a way of passing on values.

Activity

Culture is how a group of people carries out its traditions and way of life. Use four examples of Pueblo culture to create a Pueblo Cultural Handbook. First write a sentence or two for each topic. Then use images and descriptions from *The Pueblos* as guides for illustrating each topic. Make a cover for your handbook and remember to include the author's name!

Pueblo
Cultural
Handbook

by
Cara Harding

Key Concept 3 Early trade was a way of exchanging both goods and ideas.

Activity

Create a two-column chart listing the goods the Pueblos traded with other groups. Label the two columns: "Items the Pueblos Brought to Trade" and "Items the Pueblos Took Home." Include at least three items in each column.

Items the Pueblos Brought to Trade	Items the Pueblos Took Home

Write Your Autobiography

Many people like to write autobiographies, or stories of their own lives. You can write a short autobiography that focuses on three or four important events in your life. You will probably have to do some research, though. Family members and friends can help you remember details.

1. Study the Model

Look back at pages 21–26. What are the things you need to think about when writing a biography or autobiography? You will need to remember these as you write your autobiography. Now, read one of the biographies again. As you read it, make a note of the most important events that are mentioned. Look at the timeline. Make a note of the important events on the timeline.

2. Research Your Topic

You already know some important events in your own life. But there will be details about the events that you won't remember. You will need to ask your parents, grandparents, neighbors, and friends.

Writing an Autobiography

◆ Choose some important events in your life.
◆ Write about the events in the order that they happened.
◆ Use a timeline to chart important dates.
◆ Use pictures with captions to illustrate your autobiography.

Make a list of the events that you want to include in your autobiography. Then make a list of questions to ask others. Take notes on what you learn. Try to get as many dates as possible so that you can create a timeline. You may also have some photographs that you can use to illustrate your autobiography.

3. Write a Draft

Look over all the information you have. Now look back at one of the biographies again. Use it to help you write about yourself. Then tell about your important events in order. If you wish, tell about how events made you feel or what you learned from them. Be sure to use pronouns like *I* and *me*. At the end, tie the events together in a concluding paragraph. Then draw up a timeline. Write a few words about the most important events along with the dates they occurred.

4. Revise and Edit

Read over your draft. What do you like? What would you like to change? Make these changes. Then read your draft again. This time, fix any mistakes. Look for words that are misspelled. Be sure each sentence starts with a capital letter. Be sure that you have your information in order.

Events in My Life

1. Got a new little sister

2. Rode my first bike

3. Was in the class play

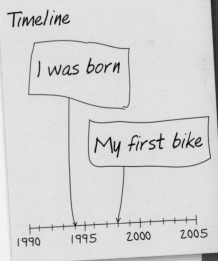

Timeline

I was born

My first bike

1990   1995   2000   2005

Publish Your Autobiography

Before you can share your autobiography, you need to publish it.

Take time to think about what your finished autobiography will look like. Do you have photographs? Where will they go? Can you keep these photographs or should you copy or scan them? Where will you put the timeline? What will you call your work? When you have made these decisions, write the final copy of your autobiography. Then you will be ready to share.

1. **Give your autobiography a title.** The title should include your name because your autobiography is your story. The title should also relate to the events you have written about.

2. **Include photographs or drawings.** Use photographs of yourself and your family, or illustrate your autobiography with your own drawings.

3. **Add captions to pictures.** Remember, captions and labels tell what pictures are about.

4. **Organize the events on a timeline.** Write a short description of the most important events next to their dates on your timeline.

Share Your Autobiography

Now you are ready to share your autobiography. Get together with a group of your classmates. Read each other's autobiographies. When you have all finished reading, discuss the things that are the same in your lives and the things that are different.

Glossary

adobe – a mix of mud and straw used to make bricks that becomes hard when dried by the sun

culture – the traditions, language, dress, ceremonies, and other ways of life that a group of people share

dialects – languages from different areas that were once the same but have changed in different ways over time

generation – all the people born around the same time

goods – products that can be bought, sold, or exchanged

homeland – the place a people or nation chooses to make its home

kivas – underground rooms used by the Pueblos for meetings and religious ceremonies

moccasins – soft leather shoes with soft soles

plateaus – areas of flat, high ground

pueblos – a Spanish word for "villages" used to name the Native American people who lived in the southwestern United States

tilled – turned over to prepare for planting

trade – the buying, selling, or exchange of products

turquoise – a type of bright blue-green stone used by the Pueblos in ornaments

Index